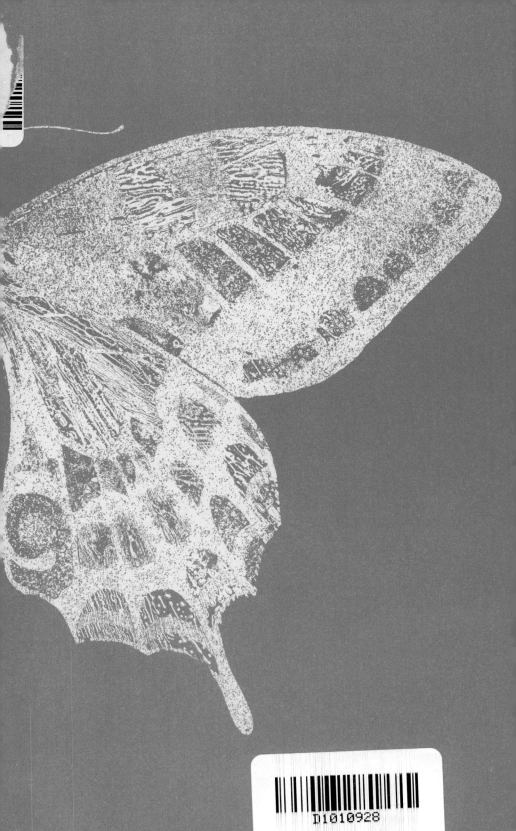

The Gift of Life

By Dean Walley
Illustrated by David Welty

👑 Hallmark Crown Editions

The maternal spirit inhabits the green forests....
....dwells in the mountains and valleys....

.... *overflows into streams and rivers....*

.... *and fills the world with love*.

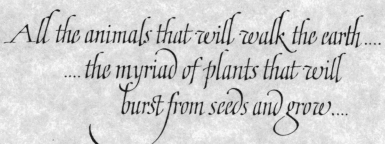

All the animals that will walk the earth....
....the myriad of plants that will
burst from seeds and grow....

....all the men and women of tomorrow
are waiting....
....waiting for the moment when
earth and heaven join in the miracle
of creation.....

The eternal soul of motherhood
radiates from the face of the earth.....
......a mother's laughter

ripples from brooks
        that race from snow-capped peaks
            to the broad rivers below.....

.... a mother's tears
fall gently
in the rain ......

*.... a mother's love shines softly
from the golden prairies
that shimmer in early evening....*

.....a mother's memories
        are reflected from silent pools
      silvered by moonlight.

Each part of nature shares the fervor of motherhood....
..... each joins in the giving of life.

A mountain pauses
in its climb to heaven.....
.........pauses to pour the waters of life
into the waiting valleys below.........

..... and in the valleys
young trees reach like arms from earth
to touch the sky.....
.... and so they are exalted.

Nature's maternal forces are as many
as the blades of grass
that carpet the earth.......

.....as varied as the faces
of wildflowers in a rolling meadow.

How like a mother is the rich earth
that nurtures a sapling in springtime.....
.....and takes the cast-off
leaves in autumn.....
only to return them, green and filled with life,
in an endless cycle of love......

Like a mother, the earth is faithful
to the seeds that wander like children
in the wind......
        she waits for them....
....patient....caring.....

and when at last the seeds settle close
to her heart, she gives them the kiss
of life.....
.....the sustenance of maternal love.

And the force sweeps
across the earth....
....to the creatures that walk....
....the birds that fly....

Each is a tribute to a miracle... a living note
in the song of life.

A mother robin attends
her hungry, squeaking brood....
....feeding....
....guarding....
....warming them under
her soft, sheltering wing.....

....while by the sparkling
stream, a doe paces nervously
along the green bank....
....silently watching over her
drinking fawn.....

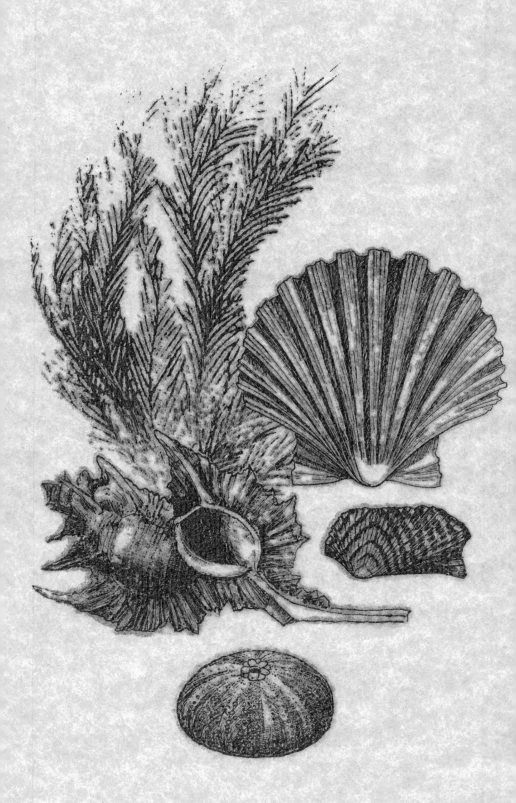

All of nature treasures the miracle
of creation....
....even the seasons turn joyfully in
their cycle....
....playing their roles, taking their places
in the enormous panorama of life.....

.....winter, cloaked in white,
bows to the growing child
that is spring.....

.....spring blossoms into summer.....

....and summer turns her riches
to autumn's gold.

And so it will be forever.
Earth will lift to heaven.....
.....heaven will descend to earth....
.....and in their meeting we will gain
.....the offering of love

.....the blessing of creation
.....the gift of life.

This book was designed and illustrated by David Welty.
The artist made his own color separations and closely
supervised the printing for utmost accuracy of reproduction.
Lettering was executed by hand and styled by Myron McVay.
The paper is Hallclear, White Imitation Parchment
and Ivory Fiesta Parchment. The cover is bound with
natural weave book cloth and Torino paper.

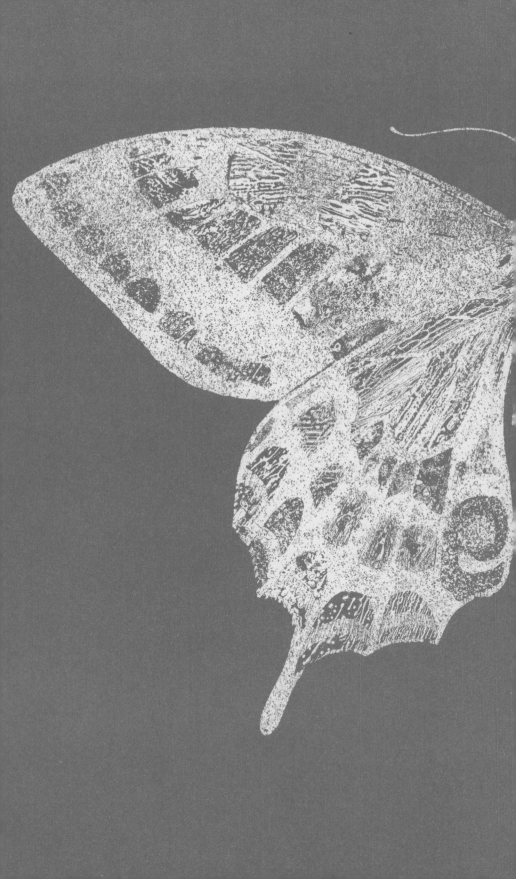